Shackled To The Sun

Noah K.N.

BookLeaf Publishing

Presentation by *BookLeaf Publishing*

Web: www.bookleafpub.com

E-mail: info@bookleafpub.com

ISBN: 978-93-95755-87-0

First edition 2022

DEDICATION

To those who don't understand

You never will so don't try to make me feel
better with those bullshit words

But read my words and know

Death is easy, living is much harder

But I did it

the moon

you tell me to search for the good in everything
to choose to be happy
to choose the light?
how can I?
how can I do that when the storm cloud called
my mind decides to destroy any and all sparks of
happiness in front of me?
how can I when the world I live in determines
my value according to my pigmentation or that
of those around me?
how can I when the darkness in the world has
declared me kin and has colonized generations
of my people in search of some sick
satisfaction?
That darkness has become a parasite that feasts
on my pain and suffering
it cuts me open with the precision of a surgeon
and leaves me to bleed out on my bathroom
floor
it leaves me vulnerable to my anxiety which
confines me to my room
my only safe place
it plants seeds of depression which can only
grow in the black of night
it blooms flowers of insomnia ao I will admire it
and when I leave my room it calls me

like a siren
and if I don't respond it comes like a strong wind
to snuff out my light and happiness
then it sweeps me up in its arms and squeezes
me until tears pour out and all of my strength is
lost

so I just lay there

the darkness seems to be the only thing that
understands
isn't that what everybody wants?
to be understood?
the darkness understands me like nobody else
like you never could
it stood by me when you couldn't so don't tell me
to look for the light
how can I not love the only thing that has been
there for me when you couldn't?

I think she knew

I was recently told that I have a mind for science
and that I should use it so that it doesn't go to
waste
When I was younger I always wanted to be a
doctor
A heart doctor, I would say
I want to fix people up
Some dogs can smell if something is wrong with
their owners like cancer or some other illness
and I wonder if child me could do the same
I wonder if she could feel my heart dying in my
chest
I wonder if she somehow knew that slow decay
would find its way through my body and lay
siege to every part I once thought was great
I wonder how many times that death had to walk
around my brain and scream until the walls
came tumbling down
I hope it was more than seven
I wonder how hard my mind is fighting not to
carve into my skin the mark of a beast that wants
to take control
I wonder how younger me was able to fight this
for so long

How she was able to mark the pain that was
hurting every part of her pain with an "I don't
know what doctor I want to be anymore"
Because that was a lie
I didn't know what part of myself needed so
urgently to be fixed anymore
I didn't know which demanded more attention
More help
Which one would benefit so greatly from being
fixed

It's not that I don't want to heal
It's that I don't know how and doctors seem to
have all the right answers
I want to be fixed
I want a transplant for my heart and my brain
and my skin and my everything
I don't want to be me anymore
I want to be something other than this body that
aches and tires and hurts

I wonder

5

I wonder why writing
My favourite thing to do becomes the only way
to get heard but I'm still not allowed to do
Because while the pen is mightier than the
sword I can't get access to either

one star

what good is one sun, one star
when there are many
all courting for your attention
wanting to be the star of the show
without the disconnect of space or time?

Maturity

Mature
Defintion
1. Fully developed physically, full-grown
2. Having reached the most advanced stage in a process
You're so mature and well-spoken, they say
You are an old soul
You're mature like you've lived a thousand lives
Mature like you have murdered yourself and come back a million times and learned more and more
Mature like you've used ink on paper to try and avoid what's going on in life
Mature like that worked for a little while but you weren't feeling productive enough by my standards
Mature like now you're addicted to stress because idle time is the devil's workshop and being busy is better than thinking about what's wrong
Mature like I don't know who I am and I become who you need me to be
Mature like all I can think about is how much I hate myself for not having a self

Mature like sometimes being alive is torture but
I can't let myself die
Mature like the death himself has made love to
me on the floor of my bathroom and told me to
let go
Mature like he did the same to my father and he
left me but laying there is the closest I can get to
him now
Mature like letting go isn't an option
So mature but not fully developed or grown I tell
you
Mature but I'm not the most advanced
Mature but I don't know what to do anymore

01/01/22

I didn't know how much I missed you
how much the grief would slowly kill me

i'm not enough

When my baby
Looks me in the eye and asks me why I didn't
fight hard enough
Fast enough
Strong enough and I can't tell her that there is a
gun to my head that isn't a metaphor that I
decided to write
I try to write fast enough
Record all my words
Tell my history
But it will never be enough
It will never be enough

atlas

do you miss it?
have your only worries be what 15+15 is?
or what you want for dinner?
I do
I miss being a kid
But was I ever really one?

03/06/22

I sit here
At his mercy
Hoping my silence is like a lighthouse
A beacon calling out to all
Praying that you'll reach my corner of the sea
and save me
I wish that you could

Never enough

13

I do my work
And I play my part
I lay in the dark of my room and realize that I
will never be safe
Even here
But what can I do?
I'm afraid to die
And I'm afraid to live
What a way to exist

what will you do?

I carved a smile into my face
and told myself the blood was simply a figment
of my imagination
I moulded myself into the ideal person
Then wondered why you put so much on me
I told myself it was me and carved my
confessions into my skin as penance and waited
to bleed out for my sins
You made me feel this way
Now your golden trophy of a child is tarnished
in your eyes
Whatever will you do?

2:40 AM

He broke my heart without knowing it
It didn't matter if our love was like the sun or the
moon
It didn't matter that he loved me more than all
the stars in the sky
He broke my heart without ever telling me how
to pick up the pieces
I kept expecting him to show up one day like an
item long forgotten
I treated him like breathing
I knew I had him but I never had to think about
it
When he broke my heart
It was like an attack
My chest hurt so bad and suddenly the air
around me didn't want to help me anymore
I had to think hard to give me what I needed ad
that was too much
So I forced it into my lungs wishing for them to
expand while all the memories of us ran down
my face
I knew what was happening and how it would
end but I didn't want to admit it
That would be too hard
Now it's been 3 years

And I still don't know how to deal with a broken
heart
I don't know how to pick up the pieces after you
left
You weren't the only person that passed that
night
I did too
You broke my heart without knowing it and you
couldn't even stick around long enough to help
me mend it
So I threw it in a box under my bed and let it sit
You weren't the only person whose heart gave
out that night but you did break mine on the way
out

03/19/22

You didn't want me
No one wanted me
So I traveled through the mail
A box shipped all around but always returned with
the following
"She isn't what we wanted"
I was fragile
It was labeled on my box
So when not handled with care I break
I learned not to put more labels
Not to scream to be careful
But I learned to duct tape myself back together
I learned that superglue will heal all those cuts and
it's easy to get
Easy to get when you shatter and no matter how
messed up you look afterwards you're still there
I'm still there
I may not want to be
But I will pick up all my broken pieces and be
thankful for the inheritance you gave me
Because even if I wish I could carve lines on my skin
to mark all the days I didn't want to survive
The inheritance you gave is all mine
And I will take all my shattered pieces and make my
reflection a reminder of the pit you thought I wouldn't
come out of

03/25/22

"A doctor" I said
"One for the heart"
A heart that beats in your chest
One that you write on cards
And paint on pictures
To showcase a love that the word love will never
be big enough to carry
What organ is more important?
This one helps you feel
Helps you connect
Helps you relate
Helps you find love to give even in the naïveté
of being a child
"Cardiology. I want to be a cardiologist." I said
Bigger words now
Now I know some things
I know that there are more important organs
The brain
The intestine
The kidney
A heart is just there but can always be replaced
Maybe there was a mistake
A piece of misplaced code
A typo
God isn't the type to make mistakes though

So maybe…
Maybe I was made to fix it
God put me here too right?
It will be my job to repair the damage
Fix what's broken
Love has nothing to do with it
At least not with you
But for my work
My specialty
The type of specialty that I will spend years
working towards and crying over
Contemplating giving up
Passing it on to someone more worthy
But it will be worth it
I will save you
I want to save you
It's my calling
My passion the thing I'm meant to do
"I want to be a cardiothoracic surgeon."
I like cutting things
A snip here
A snip there
Cutting to repair what they say isn't broken
A surgeon wants to cut
Well a surgeon I might be but not for the heart
I want to learn to cut away the parts of me that I
don't want
That you don't want

I want to stitch away all the holes I left looking
for that jackpot of pain but only finding the dirt
that you called me to be
Not in so many words maybe but isn't that what
words are for?
Interpretation?
Well i interpret that my heart is plated in gold
and flowers but the scariest cells are always the
prettiest
I interpret that The holes I make will never lead
me the pot of gold that is my suffering it will
make me feel better cause I looked
I interpret that I just don't feel like cutting out
the tumour
The parasite that is feeding on my body cause
that will mean that at least somebody wants me
I interpret that my body feels like my heart is an
imposter
That it deserves to beat in the bodies of those 6
feet under not one that is 5 feet up but has done
nothing to earn it
"Words don't bring people back to life. Maybe
2000 years ago but this is the real world where
telling your heart to beat again won't work."
I interpret that being this surgeon also means
dealing with the lungs
Hoping and praying that they won't collapse
under the pain of the simple act of breathing

Breathing in all the hatred and abuse and
breathing out the will to keep fighting
I interpret that being a heart doctor will bring me
back to the time where I had so much love to
give and not enough people to love on
But I also interpret that being a cardiothoracic
surgeon means I that will know how to cut out
my heart and drop it in a box to the bottom of
the ocean so at least the water will drown out all
my feelings
My heart is tired
And no metaphors will heal it
But by ripping it out at least it's beat will stop
And when I'm done cutting
I'll sew up the hole it left

06/21/22

Nobody noticed

I was sitting here smiling and laughing but dying
inside
All the failures and mistakes slowly digging my
grave and they said I was looking for attention
and they're right
I was looking for attention
I'm just a kid
I wanted you to notice and tell me what was
wrong so you could fix it cause I was a kid
I sat here waiting for you to tell me that it was
okay and that we were going to fix it together
You never noticed
Now while I am a functioning corpse you
wonder why I've changed
Why I seem so tired compared to how I used to
be
So lively and welcoming
You wonder why the memories of who I was
seen to have more life than the body in front of
you
When you finally notice what is wrong it
Might be too late

I've been forced into a casket of all you
should've done but didn't
You try to catch the killer not realizing that the
execution was performed because of all you
didn't do
And all you didn't notice
But that doesn't really matter, does it?
Cause it's only murder if they find the body,
otherwise it's just a missing person

blood to poison

Don't start to wonder why I've set fire to your
village
Don't wonder why I exploded and left you with
the dirt you presented to me as a luxury
Because of you the time of my clock is winding
down
Soon there will be nothing left but dust and ash
But isn't it funny that only I have to deal with the
aftermath?
Only I will have to set fire to my mind to purge
myself of all the rage you planted inside me

full blown disaster

25

I knew of inevitable death but your expectations
push me closer to supernova

08/14/22

I don't put my hands over my chest to feel it
contract and release
I don't do it because I know I won't like what I
find
And it might seem selfish of me but at least it is
me